MW00699195

A Special Gift

For

_____

From

_____

Date

_____

ISBN: 1-57051-067-9
Printed in Singapore

Mother

the Heart of the Home

Little Treasures
Miniature Books

A Child's Tea Party

A Little Cup of Tea

All Things Great & Small

Angels of Friendship

Baby's First Little Bible

Baby's First Little Book of Angels

Baby's First Little Book

Dear Teacher

Faith

Faithful Friends

Flowers for Graduation
For My Secret Pal
From Friend to Friend
Grandmothers Are for Loving
Hope
Love
Mother—*The Heart of the Home*
My Sister, My Friend
Precious Are the Promises
Quilted Hearts
Soft as the Voice of an Angel
The Night the Angels Sang
'Tis Christmas Once Again

Contents

Chapter One
MOTHER THROUGH
A CHILD'S EYES

Mother is the name for God
in the lips and hearts
of little children.
—W. M. THACKERAY

All that I am or hope to be,
I owe to my angel mother.
—ABRAHAM LINCOLN

A Mother's Prayer

Lord, give me patience
when wee hands
Tug at me with their
small demands.
Give me gentle and smiling eyes;
Keep my lips from hasty replies.
Let not weariness, confusion,
or noise
Obscure my vision of life's
fleeting joys.
So, when in years to come,
my house is still—
No bitter memories its rooms
may fill.

Jesus said, "Let the little children come to me, and do not hinder them, for the kingdom of heaven belongs to such as these."

—MATTHEW 19:14

Praise your children openly,

reprehend them secretly.

—W. Cecil

*

A babe is nothing but

a bundle of possibilities.

—H. W. Beecher

O hush thee, my babie,
Thy sire was a knight,
Thy mother a lady,
Both lovely and bright.
—Sir Walter Scott

Raising children is like making biscuits: it is as easy to raise a big batch as one, while you have your hands in the dough.
—E. W. Howe

A baby is God's opinion
that the world should go on.
—CARL SANDBURG

*H*appy the son whose faith
in his mother remains unchanged.
—ALCOTT

*T*here's only one
pretty child in the world,
and every mother has it.
—CHESHIRE PROVERB

No Substitute

$\mathcal{E}$verybody knows that a good mother gives her children a feeling of trust and stability. She is their earth. She is the one they can count on for the things that matter most of all. She is their food and their bed and the extra blanket when it grows cold in the night; she is their warmth and their health and their shelter, she is the one they want to be near when they cry. She is the only person in the whole world or in a whole life-time who can be these things to her children. There is no substitute for her. Somehow even her clothes feel different to her children's hands from anybody else's clothes. Only to touch her skirt or her sleeve makes a troubled child feel better.

—KATHERINE BUTLER HATHAWAY

The
babe at
first feeds
upon the
mother's
bosom
but is
always
on her
heart.

My Mother

My mother was the making of me. She was so true and so sure of me I felt I had something to live for, someone I must not disappoint. The memory of my mother will always be a blessing to me.

—THOMAS A. EDISON

*H*e who gives a child a home
Builds palaces in Kingdom come,
And she who gives a baby birth
Brings Savior Christ
    again to earth.

—J. MASEFIELD

"*I*sn't there one child you really
love the best?" a mother was asked.
And she replied, "Yes. The one who
is sick until he gets well; the one
who's away, until he gets home."

—ANONYMOUS

Children can have no better inheritance than believing parents. Religion can become real in the midst of the family as in practically no other way. Many of us have inherited great riches from our parents—the bank account of their personal faith and family prayers.

—Nels F. S. Ferre

Queen of Baby Land

Who is queen of baby land?
Mother kind and sweet,
And her love, born above,
Guides the little feet.

A mother's children
are portraits of herself.

—UNKNOWN

Best Friend

$\mathcal{A}$ mother's love is indeed the golden link that binds youth to age; and he is still but a child, however time may have furrowed his cheek, or silvered his brow, who can yet recall, with a softened heart, the fond devotion, or the gentle chidings, of the best friend that God ever gives us.

—CHRISTIAN NESTELL BOVEE

Her chubby hands
    crept round my neck
And whispered words
    I can't forget.
They cast a light upon my
    soul—
On secrets no one knew.
They startled me, I hear
    them yet:
"Someday I'll be like you!"
—Unknown

The sweetest sounds
to mortals given
Are heard in Mother,
Home, and Heaven.
—WILLIAM GOLDSMITH BROWN

And ye shall rejoice
before the Lord your God, ye
and your sons and your
daughters.
—DEUTERONOMY 12:12

Chapter Two
MOTHER'S FAITH

The family is the only institution in the world where the Kingdom of God can actually begin.

—ELTON TRUEBLOOD

Let parents bequeath to their children not riches, but the spirit of reverence.

—PLATO

I remember my mother's prayers; they have clung to me all my life.

—ABRAHAM LINCOLN

I don't think there are enough devils in hell to take a young person from the arms of a godly mother.

A mother is a mother still, The holiest thing alive.

—SAMUEL TAYLOR COLERIDGE

God pardons like a mother
who kisses the offense
into everlasting forgetfulness.

—Henry Ward Beecher

My son, hear the instruction
of thy father, and forsake not
the law of thy mother.

—Proverbs 1:8

Four Things

Four things in any land
    must dwell,
If it endures and prospers well.
One is manhood true and
    good;
One is noble womanhood;
One is child life, clean and
    bright,
And one an altar kept alight.

—Unknown

A Mother's Creed

I believe in the eternal importance
of the home as the fundamental
institution of society.
I believe in the immeasurable possibilities of every boy and girl.
I believe in the imagination, the
trust, the hopes and the ideals
which dwell in the hearts of
all children.
I believe in the beauty of nature,
of art, of books, and of friendship.

I believe in the satisfactions of duty.
I believe in the little homely joys
    of everyday life.
I believe in the goodness of the
    great design which lies behind
    our complex world.
I believe in the safety and peace
    which surround us all through the
    overbrooding love of God.

—OZORA DAVIS

*Y*ou get boys and girls
started right and the devil
will hang crepe on his door.

—"BILLY" SUNDAY

*N*o man is poor
who has a godly mother.

—ABRAHAM LINCOLN

Chapter Three

HOME IS WHERE MOTHER IS

A child was asked,
"Where is your home?"
The little fellow replied,
"Where Mother is."
Ah, that is home—
"where Mother is."

*B*ut every house where
Love abides
And Friendship is a guest,
Is surely home,
and home sweet home,
For there the heart can rest.

—HENRY VAN DYKE

*W*oman knows what man has
long forgotten, that the ultimate
economic and spiritual unit of any
civilization is still the family.

—CLARE BOOTH LUCE

Science has established two facts meaningful for human welfare: first, the foundation of the structure of human personality is laid down in early childhood; and second, the chief engineer in charge of this construction is the family.

—MEYER FRANCIS NIMKOFF

I Had a Mother

You may have tangible
  wealth untold;
Caskets of jewels and coffers
  of gold.
Richer than I you can never
  be—
I had a Mother who read to me.

—STRICKLAND GILLILAN

The Bible does not say very much about homes; it says a great deal about the things that make them. It speaks about life and love and joy and peace and rest! If we get a house and put these into it, we shall have secured a home.

—JOHN HENRY JOWETT

A house is built of logs and stone,
Of tiles and posts and piers;
A home is built of loving deeds
That stand a thousand years.

—VICTOR HUGO

You can no more measure a home by inches, or weigh it by ounces, than you can set up boundaries of a summer breeze, or calculate the fragrance of a rose. Home is the love which is in it.

—EDWARD WHITING

Home interprets heaven. Home is heaven for beginners.

—C. H. PARKHURST

Bless Our Home

God bless our home, and help us to
love each other true;
To make our home the kind of
place where everything we do
Is filled with love and kindness,
A dwelling place for Thee,
And help us, God, each
moment,
To live most helpfully.

—ANONYMOUS

*W*hen home is ruled according to God's word, angels might be asked to stay with us, and they would not find themselves out of their element.
—CHARLES H. SPURGEON

*W*here there is room in the heart there is always room in the house.
—THOMAS MOORE

*M*id pleasures and palaces
though we may roam,
Be it ever so humble,
there's no place like home.
—JOHN HOWARD PAYNE

*F*or the hand
that rocks the cradle
is the hand that rules
the world.
—WILLIAM ROSS WALLACE

Foundations

It is, indeed, in the home that foundations of the kind of world in which we live are laid, and in this sense it will always remain true that the hand that rocks the cradle is the hand that rules the world. And it is in this sense that women must assume the job of making men who will know how to make a world fit for human beings to live in.

—ASHLEY MONTAGUE

When my son Danny was a four-year old, we lived in a trailer. One day someone asked him, "Don't you wish you had a real home?" I was really proud when I heard him reply, "We have a real home; we just don't have a house to put it in."

— Mrs. E. Miller

A happy family is but an earlier heaven.

— Horace Bushnell

What God is to the world, parents are to their children.

PHILO

So Long As There Are Homes

So long as there are homes to which
   men turn at close of day;
So long as there are homes where
   children are, where women stay—
If love and loyalty and faith be found
   across those sills—
A stricken nation can recover from
   its gravest ills.

So long as there are homes where
    fires burn and there is bread;
So long as there are homes where
    lamps are lit and prayers are said;
Although people falter through the
    dark—and nations grope—
With God himself back of these little
    homes —we have sure hope.

—GRACE NOLL CROWELL

Love at Home

There is beauty all around
When there's love at home;
There is joy in every sound
When there's love at home.

Peace and plenty here abide,
Smiling sweet on every side;
Time doth softly, sweetly glide
When there's love at home.

Chapter Four
MOTHER'S LOVE

Her love outlasts
    all other human love,
Her faith endures the longest,
    hardest test,
Her tried loyalty through
    a lifetime proves,
That she's a friend, the noblest
    and the best.

$\mathcal{A}$nd say to mothers what a holy charge is theirs. With what a kingly power their love might rule the fountains of the new-born mind.

—L. H. SIGOURNEY

$\mathcal{M}$aking the decision to have a child—it's momentous. It is to decide forever to have your heart go walking around outside your body.

—ELIZABETH STONE

A mother's love for the child of her body differs essentially from all other affections, and burns with so steady and clear a flame that it appears like the one unchangeable thing in this earthly mutable life, so that when she is no longer present it is still a light to our steps and a consolation.

—W. H. HUDSON

Mightiest Love

The name of mother!
   the sweetest name
That gently falls on mortal
   ear!
The love of mother!
   Mightiest love
Which Heaven permits
   to flourish here.

—ANONYMOUS

Dissect a mother's heart and see
The properties it doth contain—
What pearls of love,
    what gems of hope—
A mother's heart beats not in vain.
                                    —CALEB DUNN

Maternal love: a miraculous
substance which God multiplies as
He divides it.

                                    —VICTOR HUGO

As a mother comforts her child, so I will comfort you.

—ISAIAH 66:13

The mother's heart is the child's schoolroom.

—H. W. BEECHER

What are Raphael's Madonnas but the shadow of a mother's love, fixed in permanent outline forever?

—THOMAS WENTWORTH HIGGINSON

The love of husbands and wives may waver; brothers and sisters may become deep-rooted enemies; but a mother's love is so strong and unyielding that it usually endures all circumstances: good fortune and misfortune, prosperity and privation, honor and disgrace.

His Mother

Even He that died for us upon the cross, in the last hour, in the unutterable agony of death, was mindful of His mother, as if to teach us that this holy love should be our last worldly thought—the last point of earth from which the soul should take its flight for heaven.

—HENRY WADSWORTH LONGFELLOW

There is in all this world no fount of deep, strong, deathless love, save that within a mother's heart.

—FELICIA HEMANS

Children do not know how their parents love them, and they never will 'til they have children of their own.

—COOKE

A Memory

A picture memory brings to me:
  I look across the years and see
  Myself beside my mother's
    knee.
  I feel her gentle hand restrain
  My selfish moods, and know
    again
  A child's blind sense of wrong
    and pain.

But wiser now,
  a man gray grown,
My childhood's needs are
  better known.
My mother's chastening love
  I own.

—JOHN GREENLEAF WHITTIER

$\mathcal{A}$ mother's love
perceives no impossibilities.
—PADDOCK

Chapter Five
THE WORTHY MOTHER

A Worthy Mother

Gentle hands that never weary of
toiling in love's vineyard sweet,
Eyes that seem forever cheery when
our eyes they chance to meet.
Tender, patient, brave, devoted—
this is always mother's way.

Could her worth in gold be quoted as
    you think of her today?

There shall never be another
    quite so tender, quite so kind
As the patient little mother;
    no where on this earth you'll find
Her affection duplicated;
    none is quite so fine.

Could her worth be overstated?
Not by any words of mine.
Vain are all our tributes to her,
if in words alone they dwell.
We must live the praises due her.
There's no other way to tell
Gentle mother that we love her.
Would you say, as you recall
All the patient service of her
that you've been worthy of it all?

*I*f we never have headaches through rebuking our children, we shall have plenty of heart-aches when they grow up.

—CHARLES H. SPURGEON

*M*y son, keep your father's commands. And do not forsake your mother's teachings.

—PROVERBS 6:20

Let a nation have good mothers, and she will have good sons.

—NAPOLEON

Who takes the child by the hand takes the mother by the heart.

—DANISH PROVERB

Mother's Way

Sometimes when our hearts
     grow weary,
Or our task seems very long;
When our burdens look too heavy,
And we deem the right all wrong,
Then we gain a new,
     fresh courage,
As we rise to proudly say:
"Let us do our duty bravely.
This, you know,
     was Mother's way."

If you would reform the world from its errors and vices, begin by enlisting the mothers.

—C. SIMMONS

Instant availability without continuous presence is probably that best role a mother can play.

—L. BAILYN

Hush My Dear

Hush my dear, lie still
and slumber.
Holy angels guard thy bed.
Heavenly blessings without
number
Gentle falling on thy head.

—ISAAC WATTS

When God thought of mother,
He must have laughed with satis-
faction, and framed it quickly —
so rich, so deep, so divine, so full
of soul, power, and beauty, was
the conception.

—HENRY WARD BEECHER

Mother—in this consists
the glory and the most precious
ornament of woman.

—LUTHER

The Watcher

She always leaned to watch for us,
Anxious if we were late,
In winter by the window,
In summer by the gate;

And though we mocked
    her tenderly,
Who had such foolish care,
The long way home would
    seem more safe
Because she waited there.

Her thoughts were all so full of us,
She never could forget!
And so I think that where she is
She must be watching yet,

Waiting till we come home to her,
Anxious if we are late—
Watching from Heaven's window,
Leaning from Heaven's gate.

—MARGARET WIDDEMER

Chapter Six
MEMORIES
OF MOTHER

For God, who lives
   above the skies,
Would look with vengeance
   in His eyes,
If I should ever dare despise
My mother.
      —ANN & JANE TAYLOR

None Like Her

There never was a woman like her. She was gentle as a dove and brave as a lioness.... The memory of my mother and her teachings were after all the only capital I had to start life with, and on that capital I have made my way.

—ANDREW JACKSON

Children are what the mothers are. No father's fondest care can fashion so the infant heart.

—W. S. LANDOR

Stories first heard at Mother's knee are never wholly forgotten— a little spring that never quite dries up in our journey through scorching years.

—G. RUFFINI

Despise not thy mother when she is old.

PROVERBS 23:22

A mother is...one who can take the place of all others, but whose place no one else can take.

—G. MERMILLOD

*H*e maketh the barren woman...to be a joyful mother of children.

—PSALM 113:9

The angels...singing unto one another, can find among their burning terms of love, none so devotional as that of mother.

—EDGAR ALLEN POE

It is better to bind your children to you by a feeling of respect and by gentleness, than by fear.

—TERENCE

Only One Mother

Most of all the other beautiful things in life come by twos and threes, by dozens and hundreds. Plenty of roses, stars, sunsets, rainbows, brothers and sisters, aunts and cousins, but only one mother in the whole world.

—KATE DOUGLAS WIGGIN

Love and
Pet Me Now

Take my withered hands in yours,
Children of my soul;
Mother's heart is craving love;
Mother's growing old.
See, the snows of many years
Crown my furrowed brow;

As I've loved and petted you,
Love and pet me now.
Take my withered hands in yours,
Hold them close and strong;
Cheer me with a fond caress,
'Twill not be for long;
Youth immortal soon will crown
With its wreath my brow.
As I've loved and petted you,
Love and pet me now.

—T.B. Larimore

Mother and Home

Home is the one place
in all this world where hearts
are sure of each other. It is
the place of confidence. It is
the place where we tear off
that mask of guarded and
suspicious coldness which
the world forces us to wear

in self-defense, and where we pour out the unreserved communications of full and confiding hearts. It is the spot where expressions of tenderness gush out without any sensation of awkwardness and without any dread of ridicule.

—FREDERICK W. ROBERTSON

Illustration Credits